CAMBRIDGE LIBRARY COLLECTION

Books of enduring scholarly value

Classics

From the Renaissance to the nineteenth century, Latin and Greek were compulsory subjects in almost all European universities, and most early modern scholars published their research and conducted international correspondence in Latin. Latin had continued in use in Western Europe long after the fall of the Roman empire as the lingua franca of the educated classes and of law, diplomacy, religion and university teaching. The flight of Greek scholars to the West after the fall of Constantinople in 1453 gave impetus to the study of ancient Greek literature and the Greek New Testament. Eventually, just as nineteenth-century reforms of university curricula were beginning to erode this ascendancy, developments in textual criticism and linguistic analysis, and new ways of studying ancient societies, especially archaeology, led to renewed enthusiasm for the Classics. This collection offers works of criticism, interpretation and synthesis by the outstanding scholars of the nineteenth century.

Account of the Harvard Greek Play

In May 1881, students of Harvard University performed Sophocles' masterpiece, *Oedipus Tyrannus*, in the original Greek. Witnessed by 6,000 people, this performance was reported far and wide, and has gone down in theatre history as a huge success which excited almost universal enthusiasm. Henry Norman's 1882 book commemorates the performance, providing a record of permanent value for every student of Sophocles. Norman describes the background to the decision to stage the play, and presents key information on Sophocles and the characteristics of Greek tragedy. He then recounts the performance in detail, describing the aspects of the play which made it such a memorable experience, including the music, the setting and the scholarship. The book includes a transcript of the programme and illustrations showing some of the costumes and key moments of the play. It provides a fascinating contemporary account of this landmark in the modern revival of classical Greek theatre.

T0382065

Account of the Harvard Greek Play

Henry Norman

CAMBRIDGE
UNIVERSITY PRESS

CAMBRIDGE UNIVERSITY PRESS

Cambridge, New York, Melbourne, Madrid, Cape Town, Singapore,
São Paolo, Delhi, Dubai, Tokyo

Published in the United States of America by Cambridge University Press, New York

www.cambridge.org
Information on this title: www.cambridge.org/9781108010825

© in this compilation Cambridge University Press 2010

This edition first published 1882
This digitally printed version 2010

ISBN 978-1-108-01082-5 Paperback

AN ACCOUNT

OF THE

HARVARD GREEK PLAY.

BY

HENRY NORMAN.

To have seen a Grecian play is a great remembrance.
DE QUINCEY.

BOSTON:
JAMES R. OSGOOD AND COMPANY.
1882.

TO

PROFESSOR JOHN WILLIAMS WHITE,

παρθένου φίλας φίλῳ,

THIS VOLUME

IS GRATEFULLY DEDICATED.

Contents.

Illustrations.

Note.

—◆—

THE performance of the Oedipus Tyrannus of Sophocles in the Theatre of Harvard University in May, 1881, was a memorable event in our quiet academic life. After months of preparation and anxious thought, it took us all by surprise. We had hoped to have a dignified academic performance, which should give classical scholars a vivid impression of one of those tragedies " of stateliest argument," whose full power is beyond the reach of the mere student, which might revive pleasant recollections in some whose Greek was chiefly a memory of the past, and which might perhaps also interest a few others, who would regard an ancient tragedy, like any other ancient curiosity, with kind and charitable consideration. None were more surprised at the almost universal enthusiasm which the actual performance excited — none, indeed, were more surprised at the effect of the performance upon themselves —

than those of us who should have understood best the power and grandeur of a tragedy of Sophocles. This was due in no small measure to the scrupulous fidelity with which every one who took part in the performance devoted his best strength to its success ; but it was due also, and more than to all else, to the native power of Attic tragedy, which suddenly revealed itself, even to those who were ignorant of its form and its language alike, as a veritable "possession for all time."

It is eminently proper that the first performance of a Greek tragedy in America should be commemorated in some permanent record ; and all who were interested in our play will be glad to know that this volume has been prepared for that purpose by one whose intimate relations to the play give him a special right to be its chronicler.

W. W. GOODWIN.

HARVARD UNIVERSITY,
December, 1881.

Introduction.

———◦◦⊱✵⊰◦◦———

UDDENLY, in December last, an
opportunity dawned — a golden
opportunity, gleaming for a moment amongst thick clouds of impossibility
that had gathered through three-and-twenty
centuries — for seeing a Grecian tragedy presented on a British stage, and with the near-
est approach possible to the beauty of those
Athenian pomps which Sophocles, which
Phidias, which Pericles, created, beautified,
promoted." These were the words of De
Quincey more than thirty years ago. The
opportunity was eagerly embraced, the tragedy witnessed with delight, and De Quincey

concludes his essay of forty pages with the
assurance that "it was cheap at the price of
a journey to Siberia, and is the next best
thing to having seen Waterloo at sunset on
the 18th of June, 1815," and condenses his
deliberate judgment in the words which serve
as a motto for the present volume. Such
unstinted praise awarded to an insignificant
representation of the Antigone in English
may serve as an apology, if one be needed,
for these pages. The play of which they
give an account is the masterpiece of classic
tragedy; it was produced under the auspices
and within the precincts of a great university; each detail of the presentation was in
the charge of men known for exact scholarship and literary taste; difficulty and expense
were alike disregarded in the effort to give
an impressive reproduction of an Athenian
performance; seven months were spent in
preparation. The play was witnessed by
six thousand people; on the occasion of the

first performance, by an audience which, for literary distinction, has probably never been equalled in America; many persons were unable to obtain seats, although ten times the original price was freely offered; it was reported by every considerable newspaper in the country,* and the news of its performance was not only telegraphed to Europe, but was even inserted in the local papers there, so that — owing to the difference of time — while the strains of the first choral ode were ringing through the Sanders Theatre, a Harvard man who was studying in Bonn overheard a group of German students discussing it over the *Biertisch*. These facts seem to call for some permanent record and description: it would be unfitting that an event at once so unique in its character and productive of such wide-spread interest should receive no other memorial than a niche in the limbo of pleasant memories.

* See Appendix 3.

In the statements concerning Athenian art
and literature which are necessary to the comprehension of the Harvard Greek play, the
writer presents no claim to originality. To
the committee which had charge of the play,
to whose learning and exertions its success
was chiefly due, he desires to acknowledge
his indebtedness and to express his thanks.

In addition to their interest as portraits of
the principal characters, the illustrations have
been selected to exhibit the typical costumes,
attitudes, and incidents of the play. Their
number being limited, it was necessary to
omit several portraits which might naturally
be expected. The groups and portraits are
reproductions, by the Heliotype Printing
Company, from negatives taken with great
success by Mr. James Notman, of Boston,
except the portrait of Jocasta (Mr. Opdycke),
which is by Pach. The groups were photo-
graphed on the stage of the Sanders Theatre
with the electric light; they are, therefore,

representations of the actual scenes of the
play. In comparison with the portraits,
which were taken in sunlight, they will
appear dark and somewhat indistinct; it
must be borne in mind that photographing
with the electric light is attended with many
difficulties which are not present in the ordi-
nary process. These groups of the Greek
play, of which eight are reproduced here,
are believed to constitute the most extensive
piece of photography of this kind which has
yet been attempted, and reflect great credit
upon Mr. Notman.

The illustrations in the text have been
drawn, and in several instances designed also,
by Mr. C. H. Moore, Instructor in Drawing
in Harvard University. The engraving is by
Closson.

I.

THE presentation of a Greek tragedy was no new idea at Harvard University. In 1876 the Memorial Hall was completed by the erection of the Sanders Theatre, and Professor Goodwin wished to mark the occasion by the performance of the Antigone of Sophocles in the original Greek. After a favorable reception and some discussion the plan was abandoned because of its many difficulties. The idea of a Harvard Greek play was then allowed to lie in abeyance, with an occasional allusion by some enthusiastic person, until the summer of 1880. In the mean time the Agamemnon of Aeschylus had been performed with signal success by Oxford students, and had met with the warmest reception in London. Many accounts of the Oxford play and its success had come across the ocean and had aroused the dormant desire to produce a similar play at Harvard. Some of the English newspapers have alluded slightingly to the Harvard play as another instance of the "manner in which America follows everything that is initiated in England." This is unjust, as the idea had been entertained here long before the Agamemnon was thought of at Oxford. On the other hand, the assertion in this country that the Oedipus at Harvard was an entirely spontaneous and independent movement, is equally untrue. We are indebted to England for the immediate inspiration and suggestion of the undertaking; had there been no Agamemnon at Oxford there would have been no Oedipus at Harvard.

The awakened plan took shape at the meetings of an informal philological club,

which numbered among its members several
Harvard professors. A Harvard Greek play,
— why not? This is not a country where
ideas go a-begging, so the proposal was no
sooner made than it found many warm sup-
porters; a few hearty discussions put it into
a practical shape and removed such obstacles
as had presented themselves, and the opening
of the autumn term found it a definite and
attractive scheme. A committee was formed,
the various divisions of the work to be done
were assigned to those most competent to
take charge of them, and conferences were
held with the students who would probably
be invited to take part in the performance.

With little discussion it was decided to
attempt the Oedipus Tyrannus of Sophocles.
This play was chosen, first, as the masterpiece of the classic stage, and as being typical of so many elements of Greek thought;
and secondly, because of the significance of
its plot to a modern mind, and the adap-

tability of its scenic details to modern and local conditions.

The distribution of the rôles followed immediately the selection of the play ; the chosen few bent themselves to their long task, and before the autumn term of 1880 was a month old, regular work on the Greek play had been begun.

II.

ESS than a mile and a half from
Athens stood the hill of Colonus.
Its beauties have been sung by
its own poet.

O stranger, thou hast reached the dwellings of a land
Where noble steeds are bred, — earth has no better homes —
Colonus, with a gleaming altar crowned.   Here, too,
The clear-toned nightingale pours forth her plaintive note
Down in green glades where purple ivy grows,
The ivy which she loves, and where the thicket grows
Sunless, untrodden, shaken by no winds, a fruit
Of myriad berries bearing, sacred to the God.
There joyous Dionysus wanders ever
In happy frolic with the Nymphs who care for him ;
And nourished by the falling dews of heaven each day
The clustering narcissus blooms, the ancient crown
Of mighty Goddesses ; and there its golden head .
The crocus shows.   The sleepless rills which flow
To feed Cephissus' streams are never dry, but with
Each day their quickening waters o'er earth's bosom flow.
The chorus of the Muses does not shun the spot,
And Aphrodite with her golden reins is there.

It is no wonder that the dwellers in this
favored place were proud to call themselves
Coloniatae, as well as Athenians. And another distinction was added to Colonus, which
was destined to outlast all the rest; a voice
which should ring out for ages after the
sacred groves had changed to " cold, bare,
ruin'd choirs"; a power which should live
on "to better and convert mankind" when
Dionysus had become a dream and Athena
but a vision. It was the birthplace of
Sophocles.

Never has any people reached such a
height of intellectual power, and left such a
legacy of influences that will be possessions
forever, as did the Greeks in the age of
Pericles. To guard against the suspicion of
ungrounded enthusiasm, it may be well to
recall the words of a careful scientific investi-
gator of men. Mr. Francis Galton, in his
work on " Hereditary Genius," at the close
of a discussion to establish the proposition

that " the ablest race of whom history bears record is unquestionably the ancient Greek," makes the following astonishing statement: "It follows from all this that the average ability of the Athenian race is, on the lowest possible estimate, very nearly two grades higher than our own, — that is, about as much as our race is above the African negro."

At this time the shadow of Eastern supremacy had been dissipated and " the great King" was no longer spoken of with terror. Marathon, Thermopylae, and Salamis, names of immortal memory, were in the immediate past; Greek courage, one may almost say Athenian courage, had scattered the hosts of Persia; a struggle on which the welfare of mankind depended had been won for the cause of freedom and civilization; " to the triumph of the Greeks," says Mr. Symonds, " we owe whatever is most great and glorious in the subsequent achievements of

PLATE I.

the human race." Free from fear and fight-
ing, Greece turned at once to the development of its own powers: of all the cities of
Greece, Athens was the one which had done
most for its liberation, and was the first to
take advantage of what had been so bravely
won. "She who saved me," was added to
the attributes of Athena. In a few years
Athens reached that height which has been
at once the inspiration and the despair of
all succeeding civilization. The undying
names of Greece gather around Athens at
this moment: Themistocles, Aristides, Pericles; Aeschylus, Sophocles, Euripides; He-
rodotus and Thucydides; Phidias, — all these
may be considered contemporaneous.

Although to write an account of the life
of Sophocles has been compared to the task
of making bricks without straw, enough is
known about him to have justified the most
remarkable eulogies. The facts of his life are
briefly as follows: He was born at Colonus

in 495 B. C., received a complete and typical education, and was famous as a youth for his remarkable beauty. On his first appearance as a tragic poet, in 468 B. C., at the festival commemorating the return of the bones of the Athenian hero Theseus, he defeated his great predecessor Aeschylus. During sixty years he wrote busily, composing a hundred and thirteen plays, only seven of which, with some fragments, have been preserved. Although so few in number, it is probable that the dramas which still exist are among the best he wrote; and representing, as they do, both the genius of Sophocles and the spirit of his age, they are among the most valuable literary possessions of mankind. His life embraced the whole field of human activity; nothing which could teach or strengthen a man seems to have been lacking in his experience. Auspicious in its opening, glorious in its course, his career was crowned with the blessing which the

Greeks regarded as most precious, — death
came before any misfortune had disfigured
him. He died in 405 B. C., thus being spared
by one year the sight of the subjection of his
native city and the beginnings of the down-
fall of his country. This fact is brought
prominently forward in the epitaph written
by Phrynichus, — καλῶς ἐτελεύτησ᾽ οὐδὲν ὑπο-
μείνας κακόν.

> " Thrice-happy Sophocles ! in good old age,
> Blessed as a man and as a craftsman blessed,
> He died : his many tragedies were fair,
> And fair his end, nor knew he any sorrow." *

Time and place appear to have found
their happiest combination in the creation
of Sophocles; this fact has impressed itself
upon almost every writer who has treated of
him. Schlegel says : " It seems that a be-
neficent Providence wished in this individual
to evince to the human race the dignity and
blessedness of its lot, by endowing him with
every divine gift, with all that can adorn and

* Symonds's translation.

elevate the mind and the heart, and crowning
him with every imaginable blessing in this
life." Mr. Symonds writes: "We cannot
but think of him as specially created to represent Greek art in its most exquisitely bal-
anced perfection. It is impossible to imagine
a more plastic nature, a genius more adapted
to its special function, more fittingly provided
with all things needful to its full development, born at a happier moment in the history of the world, and more nobly endowed
with physical qualities suited to its intellectual capacities." And again: "We have
every right to accept his tragedy as the
purest mirror of the Athenian mind at its
most brilliant period." With regard to this
latter point, — the most important in the
present connection, — no judgment can be
of more weight than that of Curtius, and
he gives forth no uncertain note. "The art
of Sophocles was a glorified exponent of the
spirit of Periclean Athens."

PLATE II.

It would be easy to multiply these quotations. One more must be given, both on account of its poetical beauty and of the position of its author. Matthew Arnold replies to a friend,

" Who prop, thou ask'st, in these bad days, my mind ? "

In an age when the material aspects of life crowd out the spiritual, when art is either a memory or a hope, whom does this man of culture find to guide and refresh him, to prop his soul ? His answer is : The blind old Homer much ; much the halting slave Epictetus ;

> " But be his
> My special thanks, whose even-balanced soul,
> From first youth tested up to extreme old age,
> Business could not make dull, nor passion wild ;
> Who saw life steadily, and saw it whole ;
> The mellow glory of the Attic stage,
> Singer of sweet Colonus, and its child."

So, of the hosts of prophets and preachers, of singers and workers, the one to whom this man of trained mind and pure spirit looks "in these bad days" is Sophocles.

After what has been said of the genius and representative character of Sophocles, nothing need be added to show the wisdom of selecting his composition for performance at Harvard.

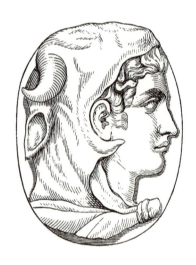

III.

BEFORE any account of the play itself can be given, some of the characteristics of Greek tragedy in general must be briefly stated. The most prominent of these is a fundamental religious character. In this respect a Greek tragedy may be compared to the passion-plays of the Middle Ages. The legend upon which it was based was as familiar to the Greek spectator as the story of the Passion is to a modern churchman. Many of the legends were derived from Homer, whose poems formed the bible of the Greeks. This would suffice to lend a solemn interest to the representation of them; and when we consider the additional facts that the tragic drama was filled with the expression of feel-

ings of intense patriotism, and that it was the
embodiment of the loftiest moral conceptions
of the age, the sacred character of the performances becomes clear. In the tragedies
of Aeschylus the nobility of mankind is
pictured in the Gods; Sophocles struck the
key-note of subsequent Greek sentiment by
exhibiting the supreme characteristics of mankind in men themselves. This prompted the
saying that Euripides portrays men as they
are, Sophocles, as they ought to be. He stood
midway between the theologic vastness of
Aeschylus and the commonplaceness — using
the word in no bad sense — of Euripides.
Hence his ethical strength and the immortal inspiration of his verse, — παντὶ μέσῳ τὸ
κράτος θεὸς ὤπασεν.

When these masterpieces of tragedy were
produced there were few readers in Athens,
but many hearers. The costs of the performance were divided between the state and
some wealthy and aspiring citizen.   There

PLATE III.

was a "theoric fund" from which the en-
trance-fee was supplied to poor citizens. The
great Dionysiac festival, celebrated once a
year, was the occasion of the performance;
thirty thousand people, citizens, — men and
women, — priests, strangers, and ambassa-
dors, formed an audience from whose size
the significance of the event may be understood. The highest honors were bestowed
upon the successful dramatist, and all the attendant circumstances united with the greatness of the plays themselves to render the
performance an occasion of intense interest.

The Sanders Theatre at Cambridge somewhat resembles the classic theatre in shape.
The stage is long and narrow, open at the
sides and top; while the seats form a series
of concentric semicircles, one above another.
Although the building does not compare in
size or dignity with the Greek theatre, it is
equally removed from the ugly outlines and
tawdry decorations of the modern playhouse.

There is no place in this country in which a Greek tragedy could be performed with less apparent anachronism.

The theatre of Dionysus at Athens was built upon the southern slope of the hill of the Acropolis, and was entirely open to the sky, an arrangement natural in such a fair and regular climate as that of Greece. The plays were performed in broad daylight, and this open-air reality added great force to the scenes. Many features of the famous Attic landscape were in sight, and the actor could make them the subjects of telling gesture. The noble farewell of Ajax illustrates the opportunities of this kind.

> "And thee I call, thou light of golden day,
> Thou Sun, who drivest on thy glorious car,
> Thee, for this last time, never more again.
> O Light, O sacred land that was my home;
> O Salamis, where stands my father's hearth,
> Thou glorious Athens, with thy kindred race;
> Ye streams and rivers here, and Troïa's plains,
> To you that fed my life I bid farewell;
> This last, last word does Ajax speak to you;
> All else I speak in Hades to the dead."

A speech like this, full of allusions to familiar and beloved places, delivered with gestures suggesting the position of each, and concluding with the death of the speaker, must have produced a profound impression.

The spectators frequently numbered twenty-five thousand, sitting on semicircular tiers of stone seats, built one above another. Front seats were reserved for priests, magistrates, and distinguished strangers. The space corresponding to the modern pit was left open, and in the middle stood the altar, or $\theta\nu\mu\acute{\epsilon}\lambda\eta$, around which the Chorus performed its sacred dance and sung the choral odes. The stage was long and narrow, the back representing in most cases a palace, which was constructed, not merely painted. The actors wore masks with strongly defined features indicating the characters they were playing. These masks were necessary to render the face visible at a great distance; they expressed the nobility of Gods and heroes, and made it possible for one actor to play several parts. It is probable that the masks contained appliances to increase the volume of the voice. Very thick-soled shoes were worn to give heroic stature, and every article of dress was so adjusted as to add to the appearance of strength and dignity. The female parts were played by men. It is important to remember that the stage right, that is, the entrance to the left of the spectators, was supposed to lead to foreign parts; the stage left, to the city, or the home of the person concerned.

The most striking and original feature of the Greek drama is the Chorus. As employed by Sophocles this consists of fifteen persons, their character varying with the circumstances of the play, but generally corresponding to the leading part. Thus in the Oedipus the Chorus is composed of Theban elders. The function of the Chorus is that of a commentary on the play: the

PLATE IV.

action of a play is given by the actors; the
reflection of a play is given by the Chorus.
They pour forth thanksgiving or supplica-
tions to the Gods; through their leader, the
Coryphaeus, they address the personages of
the tragedy to calm impetuosity or to give
courage; they utter philosophic odes suggested by the virtues or vices, the success
or misfortune, of the characters. All these
functions are beautifully exhibited in the
Oedipus.

Οἰδίπους Τύραννος, variously translated
" Oedipus Tyrannus," " Oedipus Rex," and
" Oedipus the King," is generally considered the masterpiece of classic tragedy; it
exhibits, says Professor Lewis Campbell,
" the perfect development of the various
elements of Greek tragic art." Aristotle
numbers it among αἱ κάλλισται τραγῳδίαι,
and indeed he may be said to regard it as
the type of a perfect play, since he supports most of his views on tragedy by

quotations from it. The universality of its
portrayal of men and morals — in a word,
its supremely human character — has caused
it to be imitated and translated many times.
Beside many classic imitations, Corneille,
Voltaire, La Motte, and Dryden have each
written his Oedipus, and a modern French
translation has just been produced at the
Théâtre Français. Perhaps the most surprising feature of the performance at Harvard
was the impression left upon the spectators.
Although the majority of them were unable
to follow the Greek, and were not entirely
familiar with the Greek point of view, still
the characters appealed to them so strongly,
and the ethical situation was so overwhelm-
ing, that they listened with bated breath
and separated in silence. The old Greek
spirit of the tragedy took so deep a hold
upon the more thoughtful portion of the
audience that even now, several months
afterwards, an allusion to the play is suffi-

cient to cause a change in the tone of the
conversation.

In the northern part of Boeotia stood the
ever-famous city of Thebes. Of all Greek
cities it was richest in its legendary past,
and its greatness was not diminished in his-
toric times. It was the birthplace of Dionysus and Hercules, the seven-gated city οὗ δὴ
μόνον τίκτουσιν αἱ θνηταὶ θεούς; within its
streets the strains of Amphionic music were
first heard; its varying fortunes furnished
themes to all the poets. There, in mythi-
cal, heroic times, the scene of the Oedipus
is laid. Many years before the period upon
which the play opens, Laius had been king
of Thebes. He had taken for his wife Jocasta, the daughter of Menoeceus, but no
children had been born to them, — in Greek
eyes a sure sign of the displeasure of the
Gods. In order to receive counsel and aid,
or to escape punishment, there was in those

days but one thing to be done, and Laius in his sorrow followed the usual pious custom. He betook himself to the powerful shrine of Apollo at Delphi, praying the God to grant that the race of the Labdacidae might not perish. His prayer was granted, but with a fearful addition. This is the answer of the oracle as versified by a late writer: —

"Laios, Labdacos' son, thou askest for birth of fair offspring ;
    Lo ! I will give thee a son, but know that Destiny orders
    That thou by the boy's hand must die, for so to the curses of
       Pelops,
    Whom of his son thou hast robbed, Zeus, son of Kronos, hath
       granted,
    And he, in his trouble of heart, called all this sorrow upon
       thee." *

Accordingly a son was born to the unhappy pair; but Laius, thinking to escape the terrible doom, ordered his wife Jocasta to cause it to be left to perish in the mountains. By the mother's directions the ankles of the child were pierced and tied together with a thong,

* Plumptre's translation.

and it was given to a shepherd to be hung
up to die on a tree in the most desolate part
of Mount Cithaeron. The additional cruelty
of boring the child's ankles was to make
its death doubly sure, since even if some
tender-hearted traveller should chance upon
the hiding-place, he would be unlikely, as
a Greek, to rescue and rear a cripple. The
shepherd, however, took the dangerous course
of disobeying the royal command, and gave
the babe to a Corinthian herdsman with
whom he was accustomed to share the pas-
ture. This man carried the boy to Polybus
and Merope, the king and queen of Corinth,
who, being childless, reared it as their own
son. The only trace of his mother's cruelty
remained in the swollen feet, and from this
peculiarity the name Οἰδίπους — "swell-foot"
— was given to him. The boy thus born
under a curse, thus cruelly condemned, and
thus miraculously saved, — a veritable παῖς
τυχῆς, as he afterwards called himself, — is

the famous Oedipus of Theban legend and the hero of the Sophoclean tragedy.

Oedipus grew to manhood at the court of Corinth, never doubting that he was the true son of Polybus and Merope, until one day a drunken comrade taunted him with the uncertainty of his birth. Early on the morrow Oedipus besought his supposed parents to deny this uncertainty and to prove him their son. A vague answer and the punishment of the babbler did not satisfy him, and, being unable to learn the truth at home, he too journeyed to the Delphian Apollo. The answer to the father had been terrible, but the curse lived, and the answer to the son was more terrible still. Many years later Oedipus gave this account of what the oracle told him : —

> "The God
> Sent me forth shamed, unanswered in my quest ;
> And other things he spake, dread, dire, and dark,
> That I should join in wedlock with my mother,
> Beget a brood that men should loathe to look at,
> Be murderer of the father that begot me."

Overwhelmed by this most frightful fate, Oedipus determined never to return to Corinth nor to see Polybus and Merope again, thus imitating his father's attempt to prove the God a liar, — and with as much success. Quitting Delphi he chose a road of which he knew nothing except that it led away from Corinth. Following it, he came to a spot where three ways met, the road leading from Delphi branching towards Boeotia and towards Daulia. This spot, where the ills of Oedipus began, became famous under the name of ἡ σχιστὴ ὁδὸς, — the Divided Way; in the second century A. D. the traveller Pausanias saw the heaps of stones supposed to cover the bodies of the men whom Oedipus slew. There in the narrow pass Oedipus met an old man travelling in a chariot drawn by colts. It was Laius, once more on his way to Delphi; thus father and son strangely met. The attendant leading the animals shouldered the dusty wayfarer from the path. Oedipus

turned in anger and struck him. The old
man watched his opportunity, and with his
goad dealt Oedipus a blow on the head.
The anger of Oedipus then became uncon-
trollable, — κτείνω δὲ τοὺς ξύμπαντας, he
says when describing the occurrence; "I
slew them every one." Following the road
he had blindly chosen, he came to the vicinity of Thebes, where a still more surprising
adventure awaited him. On the lofty high-
way leading to the city, the Sphinx, a monster with the face of a woman, the wings
of a bird, and the tail and claws of a lion,
had stationed herself; she seized every one
who passed, and demanded the solution of an
enigma. Those who failed to find it — and
no one had succeeded — were hurled from
the rock where she dwelt. In Oedipus she
met her match; the riddle was no sooner
propounded than it was solved, and the
Sphinx cast herself down and perished among
her victims. Arriving at Thebes, Oedipus

PLATE V.

found it in a state of the greatest excitement
and terror. The ravages of the monster had
threatened to devastate the city, and in des-
peration Creon, the successor of Laius as
king of Thebes, had offered his crown and
the hand of his widowed sister Jocasta to
any one who should destroy the Sphinx.
Ignorant alike of the peril and the promise,
Oedipus had accomplished this; he was consequently hailed as saviour by the grateful The-
bans and received the double reward. Then
came years of joy and prosperity; four children were born to the unsuspecting king;
honored as a heaven-sent ruler, and happy
as a husband and father, it is not surprising
that he forgot the days of fearful oracles and
aimless wanderings. But the greater the fan-
cied security the more dreadful the awakening to bitter reality; and the awakening soon
came. A plague fell upon the famous city,
the crops were blighted and the children
were perishing. This was the beginning of

the end, and with it the tragedy of Oedipus
the King opens.

An account of the movement of the play
will be necessarily interwoven with the description of the performance. The preceding
remarks and detailed narrative are designed
to suggest to the reader the point of view of
a Greek spectator, and therefore to aid in the
appreciation of this wonderful play. Wonderful, for it exhibits an unparalleled union
of artistic accuracy and moral power.

> " So write a book shall mean, beyond the facts,
> Suffice the eye, and save the soul beside."

IV.

E must now return from Thebes to Cambridge, and resume the narrative at the point where it was left at the close of the Introduction.

As soon as a decision was reached, the professors of the Greek department of the University undertook the work of arrangement and direction. To describe the services of each of these gentlemen would be to introduce matter of too personal a nature; it must suffice to place their names upon record as those of the persons to whom the success of the play was mainly due. Professor W. W. Goodwin, Professor J. W. White, and Professor Louis Dyer were untiring in their labors, and Professor Charles Eliot Norton lent encouragement and suggestion.

From the first the necessity of original music for the play had been evident, and the work of composing it was undertaken by Professor J. K. Paine. The task of writing music to the choruses of Sophocles — music which should preserve the original metres and embody the Greek sentiment expressed in them — was a very hard one. Little is known about the music of the Greeks; it is not probable, however, that a race which exhibited the ultimate application of the principles of several of the arts would remain contented with a barbaric music. In this modern performance two courses were open: the one, an attempt to discover the limitations of the Greek knowledge of music, and to compose, within those limitations, an adequate representation of the simpler emotions of the play; the other, to disregard the historical method, and to apply all the wealth of modern harmony and instrumentation to the expression, to a modern mind, of the varied and profound emotions which the Oedipus would rouse in a Greek breast. By the former course, the metrical structure of the choral odes would have been preserved, and consequently an imitation of the Greek orchestic movements would have been possible; these advantages would have been offset by the dulness and monotony of the music. By the latter course, while strict classical accuracy would be lost, there would be the great advantage of an additional sympathetic presentation of the great sentiments of the tragedy. Of these two courses Professor Paine chose the latter; and although there is undoubtedly room for regret that owing to the intricacy of modern musical composition the metres were obscured and the sacred dances so simplified as to be unrecognizable, still the music ranked so high as a work of modern art, and added so greatly to the comprehension of the situations and therefore to the profit of the audiences, that the final verdict must be one of satisfaction and gratitude. Professor Paine's work has been received with unqualified approval : the critic of the "Nation" ventured to prophesy that it will be "interesting to future generations as one of the landmarks in the history of musical art."

After the organization of the Harvard managers, the details were arranged with great rapidity. The play was finally cast as follows * : —

Oedipus	Mr. George Riddle.
The Priest of Zeus	Mr. W. H. Manning.
Creon	Mr. Henry Norman.
Teiresias	Mr. Curtis Guild.
Jocasta	Mr. L. E. Opdycke.
First Messenger	Mr. A. W. Roberts.
The Shepherd of Laius	Mr. G. M. Lane.
Second Messenger	Mr. Owen Wister.

* According to classic custom the characters are placed in the order in which they speak.

The rôle of Creon was originally assigned to Mr. J. R. Howe; he was compelled by a severe illness to relinquish it.

The dramatic chorus was composed of members of the Harvard Glee Club, as follows: —

FIRST TENORS : Mr. L. B. McCagg, Coryphaeus.
Mr. N. M. Brigham.
Mr. P. J. Eaton.
Mr. Howard Lilienthal.

SECOND TENORS : Mr. W. P Davis.
Mr. J. S. How.
Mr. Gustavus Tuckerman.

FIRST BASSES : Mr. F. R. Burton.
Mr. H. G. Chapin.
Mr. M. H. Cushing.
Mr. C. S. Hamlin.

SECOND BASSES : Mr. Sumner Coolidge.
Mr. Morris Earle.
Mr. C. F. Mason.
Mr. E. P. Mason.

Rehearsals commenced immediately after these selections were made. Mr. George

Riddle was Instructor in Elocution in Harvard University, and under his direction the actors began the study of their parts. The beginning was made by learning the accurate pronunciation and accentuation of the lines, and in this each man was carefully trained by the professors. The lines were then committed to memory, a scene at a time. Each scene was put in rehearsal as soon as it was committed. The men received minute instruction with regard to voice, gesture, position, entrances and exits, and all the usual technicalities of the stage. It was not long before every man knew his lines and was fairly familiar with the other details of his part.

The progress of the work was marked by various steps in its development. First, the rehearsals were transferred from the hall where elocution is studied to the stage of the Sanders Theatre. This seemed at the time an alarming advance. Then came

PLATE VI.

the first rehearsal of actors and Chorus
together. It was a memorable day when
the costumes arrived, and the scene at the
opening of the trunks was one not to be
forgotten. There were vivid exclamations
of delight from some favored man who
found himself in possession of a crimson
and gold-embroidered robe ; then a shout
of laughter as one of the *mutae personae*
(*anglice*, supernumeraries) was discovered
contemplating with rueful visage a tunic
apparently only a few inches long ; there
was the comical appearance of some man
trying on his πέτασος, and the council of
war over several pieces of stuff measuring
five feet by twelve, — were they curtains, or
ἱμάτια ? Then some one discovered the sandals of Jocasta, delicately wrapped in tissue-
paper, and much masculine wit was expended
upon them.

These costumes were prepared under the
supervision of Mr. F. D. Millet, who had

made a prolonged study of costume from
the historical and artistic points of view.
Each dress was the subject of detailed consideration, with regard to historical accuracy, the figure of the wearer, the appro-
priateness to the station he was supposed
to occupy, and even the color-composition
of the scenes in which he took part. The
performance was consequently a spectacle of
the highest order. During the last month of
preparation Mr. Millet was present at many
of the rehearsals, and was indefatigable in
his efforts to make each man appreciate the
character and capabilities of his costume.
In an excellent account of the costumes of
the play * he gives great credit to the actors.
"The experience of the Harvard students
proved how easy it is to master the use of
this apparently complicated and troublesome
article of attire," — the outer robe or ἱμάτιον.
"After a few trials the students, or most of

* The "Century Magazine," November, 1881.

them at least, made up their minds which
throw they preferred, and the variety was
left to their choice. Many of them, after a
very little practice, wore their costumes with
ease and satisfaction, and learned to arrange
them without assistance. From the first it
was decided to be an exceedingly comforta-
ble dress, and much less troublesome than
had been supposed." Every man who took
part knows that whatever skill in this respect
he acquired was owing to Mr. Millet's taste
and inexhaustible good-nature.

To commit to memory three hundred
Greek verses and a complicated musical
accompaniment was a difficult task, yet it
was accomplished by every member of the
Chorus. The musical rehearsals were in part
conducted by Mr. G. A. Burdett, a gentleman
who subsequently graduated with the highest
honors in music, and who rendered valuable
assistance to Professor Paine in the labors
of preparation.

From time to time, as new scenes were
mastered, a small company would be gathered at the house of one of the gentlemen
connected with the University, and the play
so far as learned would be rehearsed. These
entertainments were excellent breaks between
the strict privacy of the regular rehearsals
and the publicity of the performances, and
are among the most pleasant memories of
the time.

The first partial rehearsals were held
toward the end of October, 1880; for five
months they occurred three or four times a
week; for the six weeks preceding the performances there was a rehearsal every day.
At last the time came when an authoritative
public announcement of the undertaking was
necessary; previous to this the newspapers
had contained only vague and often extrava-
gant statements. The committee therefore
issued a circular * which was published in the

* Appendix 1.

leading newspapers and forwarded to those
whose support might be expected. The an-
swers exceeded the highest expectations of
all concerned; from all over the country
came letters of inquiry and congratulation.
Eighteen hours before the time appointed
for the opening of the sale a line of men
representing people who desired to buy tickets for their own use, or to speculate in
them, was formed in front of the University
Bookstore in Cambridge. Every ticket was
taken in half an hour after the sale began.
A similar spectacle was witnessed on each
occasion when additional performances were
announced. Tickets were afterwards pur-
chased of speculators for five, ten, and fifteen dollars. On the day before the last
performance, when it was distinctly understood that the play would not be repeated
under any circumstances, the proprietor of
the largest ticket-agency in Boston telegraphed to Cambridge offering twenty dol-

lars apiece for as many tickets as could be obtained. In a few instances prices much higher than this are known to have been paid.

The following item, with the editorial comment, from the "Harvard Daily Echo" of May 14, 1881, needs no explanation : —

"Prof. J. W. White will be glad to see all members of the University who are not provided with tickets to any performance of the Greek Play, on Saturday, at 10 A.M., in Sever 37, when he will furnish them with tickets to the dress rehearsal. No tickets will be sold for the rehearsal."

"The managers of the Greek Play have shown that it is their intention to give every student an opportunity of witnessing at least one performance, and they have thus silenced the only objection that has been made to their management."

The interest of the public was now thoroughly aroused, and the anxieties and hopes of the few were shared by the many. The

PLATE VII.

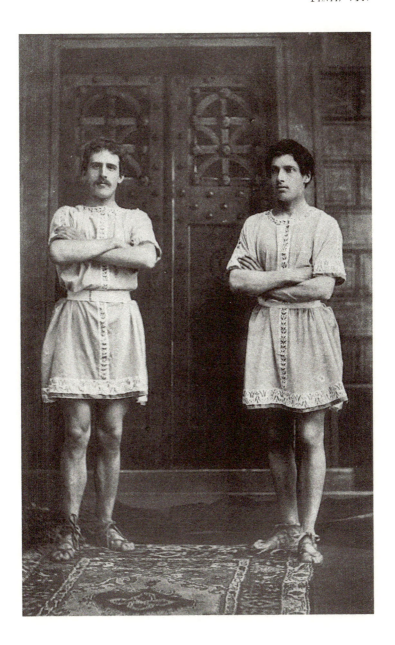

following extract from the " Boston Daily
Advertiser " may serve as an example of
the notices that appeared constantly : —

" The Greek Play to be produced next Tuesday
evening creates the greatest excitement in Harvard
circles. . . . Requests for extra performances have
been received from all parts of the State, and liberal
offers have come from New York for the play to be
given there. Tuesday night will decide its success,
and whether these offers can be accepted. The labor
of production has been gigantic, and in every way
deserving of a brilliant return."

The long period of preparation closed with
the dress rehearsal. This occurred on Saturday evening, May 14th, and was in all re-
spects similar to the regular performances,
except that no tickets were sold, and that the
representatives of the press were admitted on
the condition that it should not be reported.
As the dress rehearsal was private, no account
of it will be given. The following extracts

from newspapers representing different sections of the country will show the interest with which it was watched, and the general verdict.

From the " Boston Daily Advertiser " : —

" A full-dress private rehearsal of the 'Oedipus Tyrannus' took place at Sanders Theatre last night, in presence of a large number of invited guests, among whom were to be seen almost all the noted celebrities, literary, artistic, and scientific, known to Boston and its vicinity. The rehearsal went with a degree of smoothness that gave promise of a rare degree of excellence in the performance to take place on Tuesday evening. The effect of the costumes was extremely brilliant; the acting was unexpectedly vigorous and able; and Mr. Paine's music excited equal admiration and pleasure in its listeners. The general expression of opinion was of astonishment and gratification at the fine results attained in every essential. The whole affair, from its inception to the culmination, as seen last night, reflects the greatest credit on the taste, the judgment, and the ability of all concerned."

From the Boston " Evening Transcript " : —

" Although respect for the wish expressed by those
engaged in the production of the Greek Play at Harvard forbids us to describe or comment upon the
' dress rehearsal' of Saturday evening, we may at
least be permitted to communicate the pleasing result of that performance, — the removal of the last
doubt of a complete and memorable success. . . .
Harvard again proves herself nobly representative
of her time and country in making this most remarkable effort for art and for the drama. The labors
of those who participated in the performance must
have been as severe as they have been protracted,
and the danger of possible failure must have made it
a grave matter for all concerned in the University
not immediately enlisted in the work. But the
reward is now certain to equal the pains and the
risk, and the whole will be a delightful and honor-
able thing to remember and recount among the
glories of Harvard University."

From the " New York Sun " : —

"The end seems to have been attained as nearly
as was possible. . . . It is difficult to see how the

play could have been better rendered. It is a great honor to Harvard to have been the pioneer college in this country to achieve so arduous a work."

From the " Louisville (Kentucky) Post": —

" The first full-dress rehearsal by the students of Harvard College of the ' Oedipus Tyrannus,' in Sanders Theatre, Cambridge, Mass., on Saturday evening last, proved beyond reasonable doubt that the performance will be a success. The audience completely filled the theatre, and was very enthusiastic as well as critical, composed, as it was, of those who, from actual connection with the production, or from sympathy with the effort, are most interested and capable of passing judgment."

After the dress rehearsal there was a pause before the decisive effort. Each man spent it in adding strength at the points where he felt himself to be weak. The difficulties that had been seen had been fairly faced, and everybody had aimed high. *Le génie n'est que l'attention suivie :* the τεχνικόν had been faithfully followed; was there no reason to hope that it would be transfigured into $\theta\epsilon\hat{\iota}ov$ when the crowning moment came?

V.

THE audience gathered in the Sanders Theatre on Tuesday evening, May 15, 1881, was in many
ways a remarkable one. As was said, it has
probably never been equalled in America
for literary distinction. The familiar faces
of most of those who represent American
letters to-day were to be seen in all directions. Longfellow, Emerson, Holmes, Cur-
tis, Howells, were there; of somewhat less
distinguished men it would be easier to
name those who were absent. College
presidents and professors from all parts of
the country, several eminent magistrates,
the editors of many of the leading journals, all the instructors at Harvard, — no

branch of learning was without its distinguished representatives. Owing to the presence of ladies in large numbers the appearance of the audience was as brilliant as its
reputation.

In respect to its state of mind, also, the
audience was remarkable. Many persons
had come with doubt as to the feasibility,
or even the propriety, of the undertaking;
others thought it an excellent thing for
young men to do, but were prepared to be
thoroughly wearied; others again had come
ready to mourn the absence of the classic
glories, and to dislike what they felt sure
must be a pretentious amateur performance.
Those who were best pleased that the voice
of the old Athenian days was to be heard
again, were naturally solicitous lest some
youthful extravagance or unforeseen hitch
should mar the effect of the whole. From
the person who sat in blankest ignorance
of what was coming, to the one who had

formed all his opinions beforehand, every
state of mind was represented.   One who
carefully observed the thousand faces could
see that a doubtful and curious expectancy
was hidden beneath the universal smile.

The seats on the floor of the theatre had
been removed to make place for the θυμέλη
and the Chorus.   Outside the low barrier
which surrounded this open space sat an
orchestra of forty performers and a supplementary chorus of sixty voices.   A volume
containing the text of Professor White's
edition of the Oedipus and Professor Lewis
Campbell's translation, on opposite pages,
had been published by the committee.   The
programme (of which a reduced fac-simile
is given in Appendix 2) was an interesting
production, bearing the Harvard seal, and
printed in Greek with the exception of a
few lines of request to the audience pre-
ceded by the amusing statement, μετεφράσθη
ἔνια χάριν τῶν μὴ ἑλληνιζόντων.   The doors

were closed five minutes before the commencement of the performance.

The scene behind the long and narrow stage is the palace of Oedipus, king of Thebes, — a stately building with its frieze and columns. There is a large central door with two broad steps, and two smaller side doors; all three are closed. In the centre of the stage in front is a large altar; beside each of the smaller doors of the palace is another altar. A flight of steps leads from the stage at each side. The sound of the closing doors has warned the audience that the long-expected moment is at hand, and an immediate silence ensues. Under these circumstances the first notes of the orchestra come with great effect and the entire prelude is unusually impressive. As it closes, the spectators are sympathetic and expectant.

Slowly the crimson curtains on the right-hand side below the stage are drawn apart,

and the Priest of Zeus enters, leaning on a
staff, a venerable and striking figure.   In
Plate VI. the beauty of his drapery is seen.
Behind him come two little children.   They
are dressed in soft white tunics and cloaks,
their hair is bound with white fillets, and
they carry in their hands olive branches
twined with wool, —

ἐλαίας θ'ὑψιγέννητον κλάδον,
λήνει μεγίστῳ σωφρόνως ἐστεμμένον.

This shows that they come as suppliants.
Behind the children come boys, then youths,
and then old men.   All are dressed in white
and carry suppliant boughs ; in the costumes
of the men, the delicate fabric of the undergarment, the χιτών, contrasts beautifully
with the heavy folds of the ἱμάτιον.   With
grave attentive faces the procession crosses
the front of the stage, and mounts the steps;
the suppliants lay down their branches and
seat themselves on the steps of the altars.
The priest alone remains standing, facing the
palace door.

The first impression upon the spectators was fortunate. The innocent looks of the children, the handsome figures of the men, the simplicity and solemnity of their movements, set off as they were by the fine drapery of their garments and the striking groups around the altars, had an instant and deep effect. It is safe to say that fears of crudeness or failure began rapidly to vanish. The spectacle presented at this moment was one of the most impressive of the play; it is well shown in Plate VIII., although the groups are only partially visible.

After a short pause the great doors of the palace are thrown back, and the attendants of Oedipus enter and take up their positions on each side. They wear thin lavender tunics reaching nearly to the knee. Their looks are directed to the interior of the palace, whence, in a moment, Oedipus enters. His royal robes gleam now with the purple of silk and now with the red of gold; gold embroidery glitters on his crimson tunic and on his white sandals; his crown gives him dignity and height.

For an instant he surveys the suppliants, and then addresses them. Mr. Riddle's voice is soft and musical, and the words come full and solemn:—

       Ὦ τέκνα, Κάδμου τοῦ πάλαι νέα τροφή.

The spectators have heard the first Greek words. Descending the steps as he speaks, Oedipus asks the reason of the presence of this kneeling suppliant throng. So great is his interest, he says, in the city and its sons, that he was unwilling to learn by messengers, but has come himself, "great Oedipus, of universal fame": let this aged priest answer for them all. The old man tells the sad story of the plague. The city is again in desperate plight; Oedipus baffled the bloodthirsty Sphinx, can he not prove himself a double saviour?

" Thou, then, come,
Noblest of mortals, give our city rest
From trouble." *

This is not new to Oedipus; indeed, as
ruler, he has borne a triple grief. Many
plans for relief have been already tried; lat-
est and best, he has sent Creon, the brother
of his queen, to the oracle at Delphi to learn
in what way the city may be saved; and it
is already more than time for him to return.
While Oedipus is speaking, the children on
the left of the stage have descried some one
approaching, and one of them has pointed
him out to the priest. It is Creon, who enters
with rapid strides, wearing a wreath of bay
leaves sparkling with berries, the symbol of a
favorable answer. He is dressed in the short
salmon-colored tunic and crimson cloak, with
hat and staff. A hasty greeting follows; and
Oedipus, the priest, and the suppliants wait
for the answer of the oracle. Creon judges

* The quotations, with few exceptions, are from Professor
Lewis Campbell's translation of the Oedipus.

it best not to speak out before so many
people.

> " My message is, that even our woes,
> Borne right unto their issue, shall be well."

This is the moment represented in Plate
VIII.

The eagerness of Oedipus brooks no such
ambiguity, so Creon speaks clearly. The
oracle has declared that the plague will cease
when those who murdered Laius, and are
still dwelling in the land, shall have been
punished by banishment or death. Oedipus
then questions Creon concerning the particu-
lars of the death of Laius, and is informed
that he started on his journey to Delphi and
never returned; that an attendant arrived
and reported that the rest of the party had
been slain by a band of robbers. But why,
asks the king, did you not pursue and punish the wretches? Creon pauses and glances
round the theatre, and in the hush which follows he approaches Oedipus and utters the

PLATE VIII.

word which recalls at once the suffering of
the city and the services of him addressed:
ἡ ποικιλῳδὸς Σφίγξ, — "the riddle-singing
Sphinx," — and the harsh word echoes
through the silent theatre. "Good!" says
Oedipus, his pride gratified and his ambi-
tion roused; "then I will find them out."
With the assurance of speedy aid he leads
Creon into the palace, and the attendants
follow and close the doors. Slowly the
white-robed suppliants rise; the petition
being granted, each one takes his bough,
and led by the priest they descend the steps
and disappear.

As the last figure passes out of sight the
notes of the orchestra are heard once more,
this time with a measured beat which instantly attracts attention, and the Chorus of
old men of Thebes issues from the same
entrance. They are men of various ages,
dressed in tunics reaching to the instep and
full ἱμάτια, of harmonious soft warm colors.

The excellence of the costumes was marked;
each man seemed to have worn his dress for
years, and to exhibit his individuality in the
folds of it. They enter three deep, march-
ing to the solemn beat of the music; and
as the first rank comes in sight of the audience the strains of the choral ode burst from
their lips.

Shoulder to shoulder and foot to foot the
old men make their way to the altar on the
floor of the theatre and take up their positions around it.* This entrance of the Chorus was surpassed in dramatic effect by few
features of the play: the rhythmical move-

* In Plate IX. the general appearance of the Chorus is well
shown, although the effect of the picturesque grouping is lost,
it being necessary to crowd the men together in order to bring
so many faces within the focus of one lens. A certain peculiar
expression is accounted for by the fact that a very brilliant
electric light was suspended in front of them. The Coryphaeus is the tallest figure of the group.

PLATE IX.

ments, the coloring and drapery, the dignity
of the faces, the impressive music sung in
unison by the fifteen trained voices, — all
these combined to produce a startling effect
on the audience.

The chorus represents the citizens summoned by Oedipus to hear of his determination to investigate the murder of Laius. They
are singing in appeal to Apollo and Athena,
praying that this day may see the end of the
woes of Thebes.

" Kind voice of Heaven, soft-breathing from the height
  Of Pytho * rich in gold to Thebè bright,
            What wilt thou bring to-day ?
            Ah, Delian Paean, say !
My heart hangs on thy word with trembling awe :
What new-given law,
Or what returning in Time's circling round
Wilt thou unfold ?   Tell us, immortal sound,
Daughter of golden Hope, we pray, we pray ! "

          " And swiftly speed afar,
            Wind-borne on backward car,
   This shieldless war-god † with loud onset sweeping,

        * Delphi.
        † The plague, — " the unarmed Mars."

> To oarless Thracian tide,
> Or ocean chambers wide,
> Where Amphitritè lone her couch is keeping.
> Day ruins what night spares ; O thou whose hand
> Wields lightning, blast him with thy thundering brand."

The strophes in this ode are sung by the dramatic chorus only, the antistrophes by the dramatic chorus and the supplementary chorus together.

As the music ceases, Oedipus enters. He reiterates his determination to secure and punish the murderer of his predecessor. If any one knows aught, let him speak out; Oedipus calls down curses on the heads of those who, knowing of the matter, are silent, and bitterly curses the murderer himself.

> " Let his crushed life
> Wither forlorn in hopeless misery.
> And I pray Heaven, should he or they be housed
> With mine own knowledge in my home, that I
> May suffer what I imprecate on them."

The days of dark oracles and strange adventures are indeed forgotten, and Oedipus

thinks of himself only as the worshipped ruler
of a mighty city. All these woes, as a Greek
audience knew well, Oedipus was calling
down upon himself. They would perceive
with awe the first suggestions of the fulfilment of fate.

By the advice of Creon, Oedipus has summoned a famous seer, the blind Teiresias, a
man who holds direct communion with the
Gods. At this moment Teiresias enters, a
towering, venerable figure, with long white
hair and beard. He is guided to the stage
by a boy, whose blue cloak contrasts with
the snowy draperies of the old man. Plate
IV. is an excellent portrait.

To him

> " whose universal thought controls
> All knowledge and all mystery, in heaven
> And on the earth beneath,"

Oedipus reverently appeals. In Teiresias lies
the only hope of the city: it is a privilege
to use the power one has for good.

" Thou, then,
Withhold not any word of augury
Or other divination that thou knowest,
But rescue Thebè, and thyself, and me,
And purge this dire pollution of the dead."

Plate X. represents the scene at this moment.

The first words of Teiresias, in Mr. Guild's deep voice, take the spectators by surprise. φεῦ, φεῦ, — " Ah me ! ah me ! "

" Terrible is knowledge to the man
Whom knowledge profits not.   This well I knew,
But had forgotten.   Else had I ne'er come hither."

He knows all the truth and foresees the horror which would follow his words.   He begs to be sent home again, and counsels Oedipus to seek no farther.   The king is bitterly disappointed, and his ever-ready anger rises.   He has implored, he now threatens ; Teiresias declares that nothing shall induce him to speak.   This is one of the grand scenes of the play : two powerful

PLATE X.

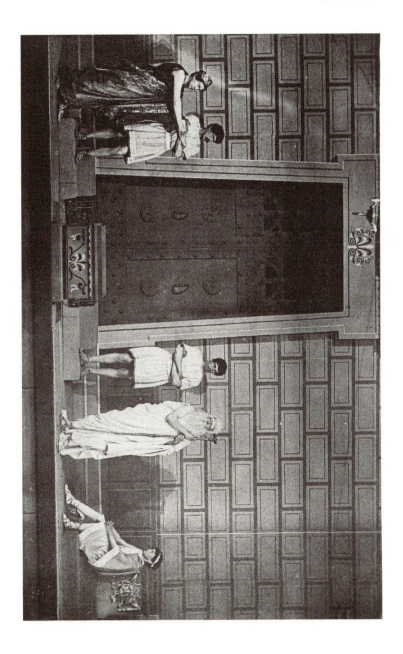

natures are in conflict; the spectators are
greatly moved by the contrast between the
passion of the king and the determination
of the seer. Which will conquer? It is the
fate of Oedipus to bring down woes upon his
head, and now he declares that he sees in
Teiresias the abettor of the murder.

> " If thou hadst eyes,
> Sole murderer had I declared thee too."

This is more than the old man can bear;
that he, the favored of the Gods, a prince
and priest, should be thus reviled by the
sinner whom he is trying to shield, makes
further silence impossible.

> " Is 't possible? I charge thee to abide
> By that thou hast proclaimed; and from this hour
> Speak not to any Theban or to me.
> Thou art the foul polluter of this land."

Roused by the intensity of his own utter-
ance, the old man goes on to declare that
the other things prophesied by the oracle

have come true, and that all men will soon
reproach the sinner. Fearful words are
these: the attendants start forward, and the
frightened Chorus gather near the stage. It
would seem that so terrible and direct an
accusation would instantly remind the king
of the prophecy at Delphi and the event
which followed. But Oedipus is blinded by
his anger, and pays no heed to what seem
lying words. So the blind man sees, and
the man whose outer sight is clear is lost in
the blindness of his soul. Oedipus recalls at
this moment the fact that it was by Creon's
counsel that Teiresias was summoned : what
is clearer than that they are together plotting
against the throne ? So he denounces them
both, and threatens punishment; if Teiresias
were not an old man he should receive it
on the spot. Teiresias calls the boy to lead
him away, but before going he prophesies
the farther fate of Oedipus in a terrible
speech: —

" I tell thee this : the man whom thou so long
  Seekest with threats and mandates for the murder
  Of Laius, that very man is here,
  By name an alien, but in season due
  He shall be shown true Theban, and small joy
  Shall have therein ; for blind, instead of seeing,
  And poor, who once was rich, he shall go forth
  Staff-guided, groping, o'er a foreign land.
  He shall be shown to be with his own children
  Brother and sire in one, of her who bore him
  Husband at once and offspring, of his father
  Bedmate and murderer.   Go ; take now these words
  Within and weigh them ; if thou find me false,
  Say then that divination taught me nothing." *

The two men part in deadly anger, Oedipus
going within the palace and the boy leading
Teiresias down the steps.   The scene was
admirably acted, and the significance of it is
vividly present to the audience ; for the first
time the performance is interrupted by prolonged applause.

Once more the music sounds, and the Chorus gives voice to its feelings concerning the
strange scene which has just been enacted.

* Symonds's translation.

At first the music is weird, and expresses
horror and anxious doubt.

> " Whom hath the mystic stone
>   Declarèd to have done
> Horrors unnamable with blood-stained hand ?
>   With speed of storm-swift car
>   'T is time he fled afar
> With mighty footsteps hurrying from the land.
> For, armed with lightning brand,
> There leaps upon his track the son of Jove,
> And close behind the unerring Destinies move."

Toward the close of the chorus the music
becomes expressive of hope, and the last
bars symbolize the confidence in Oedipus
which the words express.

> " Zeus and his son
> Know surely all that o'er the world is done :
>   But that the seer
>   Hath wisdom clear,
> Or more endowment than the crowd,
> Was never yet with evidence allowed.
>   A man with wit
> May pass the bound another man hath won ;
> But never, till I see fulfilment fit,
>   Will I confirm the blame
>   They cast upon his name.

Wise he was found beneath the searching sun,
And kind to Thebè, when the Sphinx came forth
And sang. My heart shall never doubt his worth."

As the strains of music die away Creon is
seen hastily ascending the steps on the right.
He is no longer dressed as a traveller, but in
garments suited to his high rank. His tunic
is of delicate dark crimson material, with a
gold border; his ἱμάτιον is of bright crimson
cashmere, with a broader gold border; his
sandals are of crimson and gold. He strides
to the centre of the stage and bursts out in
indignant denial of the charges that Oedipus
has made against him.

While the Chorus, through its leader, is
endeavoring to moderate the indignation of
Creon, Oedipus enters from the palace. At
such a meeting a quarrel is inevitable. The
king does not hesitate to begin it : —

" Insolent, art thou here ? Hadst thou the face
To bring thy boldness near my palace-roof,
Convicted of contriving 'gainst my life
And laying robber hands upon my state ? "

For some time Creon maintains the calm
of innocence, and asks but to be allowed to
speak in his own defence : —

"First on this very point, hear me declare " —

" I will not hear that thou art not a villain,"

is the contemptuous interruption of the king,
who nevertheless listens, though with mani-
fest impatience, to Creon's long and logical
defence. "How absurd," argues Creon, "to
suspect me of trying to supplant you! I am
much better off as I am; I have the privileges and pleasures of royalty without its
cares. Go to Delphi and satisfy yourself
that I brought back the true answer. Thus
to cast off a faithful friend is worse than
folly."

The Chorus, too, advises the king that
"swift is not sure in thought." But it is not
in the nature of Oedipus to listen to counsels
of moderation; resuming his extreme tone he
declares that Creon shall die. Creon is star-

tled out of his forced calmness, and a sharp
altercation ensues. Just as this reaches its
height the doors of the palace are seen to
open, and the Chorus bids both angry speak-
ers cease, as Jocasta is approaching. The
attendants of Jocasta enter and place themselves on each side of the door, and a moment later the queen herself stands upon the
threshold. Oedipus turns to her with welcome, and Creon with a gesture of appeal.*

* Plate XI. shows the stage at this moment. In the article
to which reference has previously been made, Mr. Millet bases
the explanation of his scheme of costume upon this scene. He
says : —

" It was part of the original scheme that in each group the
most prominent character should, as far as possible, be the
focus, not only of interest in the text, but from the point of
view of costume. Let us see how the first complex group ful-
filled this condition. On the stage left stood Oedipus, in rich
but deep-toned red ; on the right, Creon, equally in red, but of
a color entirely different in scale ; the attendants of the king,
in lavender tunics bordered with gold-embroidered white,
flanked the doorway ; and the two attendants of Jocasta, in
delicate blue and salmon, brought the eye by a pleasing gradua-
tion in intensity of color and strength of tone up to the figure
of the queen, clothed in lustrous and ample drapery."

Her dress consists of a richly trimmed silvery undergarment, and an ἱμάτιον of crimped pale yellow silk. She wears a crown, bracelets, and necklace, and white sandals embroidered with gold.

No man can hope to assume all the grace of a female figure, nor can any costume make a man look entirely like a woman. It must be said, however, that the appearance of Mr. Opdycke was charmingly feminine, and that the grace of his movements was remarkable. His assumption of a very difficult rôle was such as fully to reward a long and faithful study, and to justify the hearty praise with which his acting was received.

The first words of Jocasta are a disappointment to both the men who welcome her appearance. She has heard their angry voices, and has come to silence them : —

> " Unhappy that ye are, why have ye reared
> Your wordy rancor 'mid the city's harms ?
> Have you no shame, to stir up private broils

PLATE XI.

In such a time as this ? Get thee within !
And thou, too, Creon ! nor enlarge your griefs
To make a mountain out of nothingness."

This speech of Jocasta is followed by a *kommos*, that is, a passage in which the song of the Chorus alternates with the spoken words of the principal characters. The Chorus appeals to Oedipus to spare Creon, who has always shown himself wise, and has now hallowed by an oath his denial of the charges. At the prayer of his people Oedipus yields : Creon may go, but hatred shall follow him.

" Let me alone, then, and begone ! "

" I go,
Unchanged to these, though I have found thee blind."

And with a gesture of reproach Creon turns and leaves the stage.

Jocasta now demands the cause of the quarrel, and is informed by the king that Creon and a knavish soothsayer have accused him of the murder of Laius. Such fears, Jocasta says, are soon quieted; " no mortal

thing is touched by prophecy." Did not the
oracle declare that Laius should perish by
the hands of his own son ? Yet he was slain
by robbers at a place where three ways
meet, and the child perished in the wilds of
Cithaeron.

> " So Loxias neither brought upon the boy
> His father's murder, nor on Laius
> The thing he greatly feared, death by his son.
> Such issues come of prophesying words,
> Therefore regard them not."

One of the expressions of Jocasta has roused
strange memories in the king. "Where three
ways met," that was where he slew the traveller. "Where was this place?" he asks. "It
was in Phocis, and the roads lead to Daulia
and to Delphi." "How long ago?" "Just
before you appeared, to save the state."
"Yes; tell me how Laius looked." "He was
tall, with gray hair; in figure much like you."
"Yes, yes. Tell me one thing more. Was
he alone, or attended?" "There were five

in all, one a herald, and Laius rode in the chariot."

"Woe! woe! 'T is clear as daylight."

From the excited questions of Oedipus and the careful replies of Jocasta, anxious only to dispel all fears, one thing is proved: Oedipus is the murderer of Laius. A single slender hope remains; the attendant who escaped reported that Laius had been slain by "robbers." Should he still assert this, Oedipus is saved from the guilt of being the polluter of the state.

"One man and many cannot be the same."

Jocasta knows nothing of the youth of Oedipus, of his journey to Delphi, and of his adventure in the cross-roads; she is therefore at a loss to understand his fears. So Oedipus tells the whole story as it has already been described. It is a long, passionate speech, and Mr. Riddle's rendering is clear and powerful. The climax is reached when Oedipus, in a voice at once triumphant and remorseful, shouts, " I slew them every one." Instantly his demeanor changes, all the triumph drops from his tone, and he cries piteously, —

> " Now if there be
> Aught of connection or relationship
> Between yon stranger and King Laius,
> What wretch on earth was e'er so lost as I ? "

Jocasta again comforts him by showing that should the attendant now assert that the party was attacked by one man, still the oracle would be proved false, as it had declared that her son should kill Laius, and the babe had perished long before. Oedipus catches at the crumb of comfort, and they go within.

The choral ode which follows is one of great beauty. It begins with a prayer for purity of life, and reverence of thought and speech.

"Deep in my life, by Fate impressed,
Let holiness of word and action rest,
And sinless thought, by those Eternal Laws
Controll'd, whose being Heaven alone did cause."

The second strophe is a protest against
impiety, suggested by the impious words of
Jocasta.

"Who walks disdainfully with hand or tongue,
Not fearing acts of wrong,
Nor reverencing each temple's holy shrine?
A horrid fate be thine,
For thine abandoned greed,
Who seekest gain beyond thy rightful meed,
Nor sparest things divine,
And in thy madness touchest things accurst.
Who, when such crimes have burst,
Can look for shelter from the wrathful shower?
If such a spirit be in power,
And gilded with preferment still advance,
What means my service in the sacred dance?"

As the chorus closes, Jocasta enters in
a new state of mind. She has comforted
Oedipus by ridiculing all oracles; but she
is not without faith in the power of the
Gods, and she brings frankincense and gar-

lands, and lays them with a prayer upon
the altar.

While she is speaking, an old man has
entered on the left below the stage. He is
dressed as a common traveller, in a tunic and
short cloak, his hat slung over his shoulder, and a stout staff in his hand. It is the
messenger from Corinth. He looks round as
if in search of something, and as soon as the
queen has finished her prayer he inquires of
the Chorus where the home of Oedipus, or,
better still, the king himself, can be found.
He is promptly informed that the mansion
he sees is the palace of Oedipus, and that
the lady before it is the queen. With a profound salutation as he ascends to the stage,
he declares himself to be the bearer of news
at once good and bad. Old Polybus, king of
Corinth, is dead, and the citizens are about
to make Oedipus king. This is indeed
news to Jocasta. Oedipus has long avoided
Corinth lest he should slay his father, Poly-

bus; now he can return, as king, all fear
dispelled.

"Voices of prophecy! where are ye now?"

Oedipus enters in response to her sum-
mons. His royal robes have been exchanged
for simpler ones of white and gold. He, too,
learns the news with triumph.

"Ah! my Jocasta, who again will heed
The Pythian hearth oracular, and birds
Screaming in air, blind guides!"

One dark thought, however, cuts his exul-
tation short. He need no longer fear to be
his father's murderer, but there is a second
horror in his fate; his mother, Merope, still
lives at Corinth, and while she lives he dares
not return. The messenger, rejoicing in the
good news he brings, and hoping for propor-
tionate reward, makes bold to ask the reason
of these fears. On learning it, a smile full
of meaning crosses his face. Is this the only

thing that the king dreads? Then let him
put it aside,

> "Because with Polybus thou hadst no kin."
>
> "Why? Was not he the author of my life?"
>
> "As much as I am, and no more than I."
>
> "How can my father be no more to me
> Than who is nothing?"
>
>   "In begetting thee
> Nor I nor he had any part at all."

The old man smiles broadly at his own
humorous way of telling this good news. It
is not every one who is privileged to remove
a king's fears. And he proceeds to tell how
he gave Oedipus when a babe to King Polybus, having received him from one of the
shepherds of Laius, who had found him in
the wilderness of Cithaeron. He tells of the
cruel thong, and alludes to the scar on the
king's ankles.

But Jocasta? At the other end of the
stage the queen is writhing in anguish. The
deep-red cloak which she wears is twisted

about her; now she flings her hands up and seems about to speak, then her hands are pressed on her mouth to stop the cries which rise, or on her bosom to silence the beating of her heart. She rushes toward the king, but stops half-way; her face shows the tortures of her soul. The truth is all too clear to her. The spectator feels that this suspense cannot last, and relief comes when the Chorus suggests that perhaps Jocasta can tell something about the shepherd of Laius. When appealed to by Oedipus, she forces the suffering from her face and turns with a smile.

> "What matter who? Regard not, nor desire
> Even vainly to remember aught he saith."

But Oedipus has gone beyond recall. Her last appealing words are scorned, and with the language and the gesture of despair she rushes from the stage.

> "O horrible! O lost one! This alone
> I speak to thee, and no word more for ever."

The Chorus expresses the feelings of the startled spectators : —

> " Oedipus, wherefore is Jocasta gone,
>   Driven madly by wild grief ?   I needs must fear
>   Lest from this silence she make sorrows spring."

> " Let her !   Yet I will choose to know my birth."

In the song which follows, the Chorus indulges in fanciful speculations concerning the parentage of Oedipus. The tenor solo in the antistrophe was sung by Mr. George L. Osgood.

As the music ceases the attendants of Oedipus appear at the entrance on the right, supporting a strange figure between them. It is an aged man, with grizzled hair and beard, clothed in coarse homespun cloth, and with a rough, untanned sheepskin over his shoulders. He supports himself on a sapling staff which he has cut in the woods. He mounts the steps with difficulty, and faces the king. He is no stranger to the errand on which he

PLATE XII.

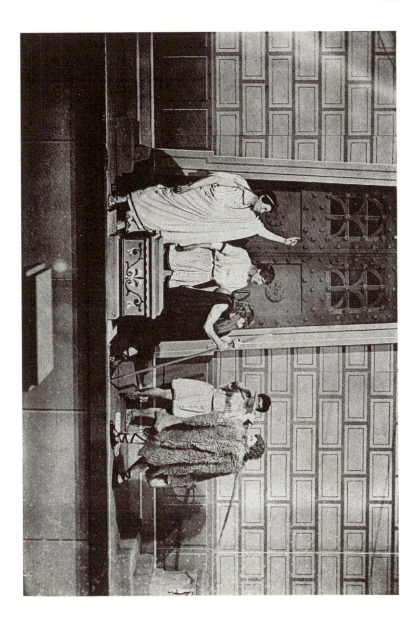

has been brought, and with the greatest difficulty he is made to speak. The contrast
between the eagerness of the messenger from
Corinth to tell all he knows, and the silence
of the tender-hearted old shepherd is very
striking. The shepherd cannot bear the other's telltale chatter, and with the words, "Con-
fusion seize thee and thine evil tongue!" he
swings his staff to strike him. The scene
at this moment is shown in Plate XII. At
a gesture from Oedipus the attendant stops
the blow. The old man must be made to
speak.

> "Thou wilt not speak to please us, but the lash
> Will make thee speak."
>
>   "By all that 's merciful,
>   Scourge not this aged frame!"
>
>   "Pinion him straight!"

And the muscular attendants spring forward
and seize him. Then the truth is wrung from
him, word by word. He gave the child to
the Corinthian; it came from the palace;

they said it was the son of Laius; Queen
Jocasta herself placed it in his hands; they
said that an oracle had declared that it
should kill its father.

> " What then possessed thee to give up the child
>   To this old man ? "

> " Pity, my sovereign lord !
> Supposing he would take him far away
> Unto the land whence he was come.   But he
> Preserved him to great sorrow.   For if thou
> Art whom he gives thee out, be well assured
> Thou bear'st a heavy doom."

The portrait — Plate V. — represents the
shepherd at this moment.

The truth is out; the oracles are not falsi-
fied ; his father's murderer, his mother's husband, Oedipus faces his doom.   With a fearful, choking cry he pulls his robes over his
head and face, and bursts into the palace.

> " Woe ! woe ! woe ! woe !   All cometh clear at last."

How great the irony of fate !   As Jocasta,
in her attempts at comfort, suggested the

PLATE XIII.

"place where three ways meet," so the Corinthian messenger, in filling, as he thinks, the
measure of the king's joy, utters the words
which damn.

"So from that spring whence comfort seemed to come,
    Discomfort swells." *

And how superbly Sophocles has pictured it!
The passionate and haughty king, flinging
his imprecations in heedless wrath, is overwhelmed by their recoil.

    "By most righteous doom,
Who drugged the cup with curses to the brim,
Himself hath drunk damnation to the dregs."

This scene — shown in Plate XIII. — was
the dramatic climax of the play.   The acting
led up to it gradually by the excited conversation and the shepherd's blow.   When
Oedipus burst through the doors of the palace,
his attendants quickly followed him; the hor-
ror-stricken messengers turned with despair-

* Macbeth : quoted by Campbell.

ing gestures and descended the steps, the
one to the right, the other to the left, and a
profound silence fell upon the theatre.

In the opening strains of the last choral
ode, which now ring out, the emotions of
the scene are wonderfully expressed. Each
one recognizes the solemnity and depth of
his own feelings in their pathetic tones.

The theme is one which Solon made famous,
— until death no man's life can safely be
called happy.

> " O tribes of living men,
> How nothing-worth I count you while ye stand !
>   For who of all the train
>   Draws more of happiness into his hand
>   Than to seem bright, and seeming, fade in gloom ?"

As the ode closes, the palace doors are
opened violently from within, and the second messenger rushes on the stage. He is
a servant from the palace, clad, like the at-

tendants, in a short light tunic. He brings
a tale of horror: Oedipus, on entering, had
called for a sword, and demanded to know
where Jocasta was. No one would tell him;
but at last, seeing the doors of the bedcham-
ber shut, he had broken through them and
disclosed the body of the queen hanging
by the bed. Tearing down the body, he
had snatched from the shoulders the golden
clasps and had thrust them into his eyes,
saying, —

> " Henceforth they should not see the evil
> Suffered or done by him in the past time,
> But evermore in darkness now should scan
> The features he ought never to have seen."

In a moment Oedipus himself appears, leaning on his attendants, his pale face marred
by bloody stains. The dismayed Chorus
hide their faces in their robes, and the king's
voice is broken with sobs as he cries, αἰαῖ,
αἰαῖ, δύστανος ἐγώ. The lament of Oedipus
is given by Mr. Riddle with great power;
the ringing Greek syllables grow more and

more impressive, and the haggard, blood-
stained face grows more terrible.

> ἰὼ σκότου
> νέφος ἐμὸν ἀπότροπον, ἐπιπλόμενον ἄφατον,
> ἀδάματόν τε κ ὶ δυσούριστον ὄν.

> " O cloud of dark, on me
> Sent loweringly !
> Hideous, unutterable,
> Invincible !
> Too surely wafted on."

In the ensuing dialogue between Oedipus
and the Chorus, the king pictures all the ill
he has done and suffered; father, mother,
children, the three ways, Cithaeron, Thebes,
the oracles, — he spares himself no bitter
memory. The closing passage of his long
lament is perhaps the most fearful thing in
any literature.

> ὦ γάμοι γάμοι,
> ἐφύσαθ' ἡμᾶς, καὶ φυτεύσαντες πάλιν
> ἀνεῖτε ταὐτὸν σπέρμα, κἀπεδείξατε
> πατέρας, ἀδελφούς, παῖδας αἷμ' ἐμφύλιον,
> νύμφας, γυναῖκας, μητέρας τε, χὠπόσα
> αἴσχιστ' ἐν ἀνθρώποισιν ἔργα γίγνεται.

PLATE XIV.

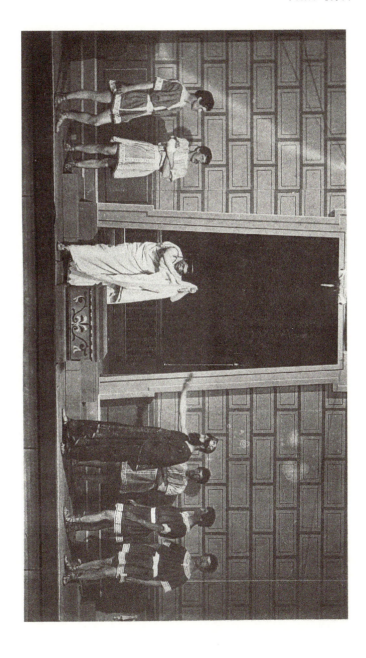

As Oedipus is begging to be slain or
thrust out of the land, the approach of Creon,
who has resumed his royal powers, is announced. The memory of all his injustice to
Creon overwhelms Oedipus, and he cannot
bear to meet him. But he is blind and unable to flee, so he hides his face and waits in
silence. Creon enters, crowned, followed by
two attendants. (See Plate XIV.) His first
words are reassuring; the new king does
not come with mocking or reproach, but
directs that a sight so offensive to earth and
heaven be hidden within the palace. Oedipus asks the boon of banishment, but is
informed by the cautious Creon that the God
must be consulted. Then the blind man
begs that his wife be buried decently, and
reiterates his prayer that he may be permitted to leave the city which he has af-
·flicted. And one thing more he asks, —
that he may embrace his daughters again.
By a sign Creon despatches his own at-

tendants to bring them, and while Oedipus
is still speaking their voices are heard.

Antigone and Ismene now enter, led by
the attendants of Creon, and are placed in
the arms of Oedipus, who falls on his knees
beside them, and addresses them with saddest
words. The children are too young to appreciate the horror of the scene, but they are
filled with pity for their father's pain. There
is a look of genuine sympathy on the two
bright faces which watch the kneeling figure.
Creon has retired to the right of the stage
and has wrapped his robe round him, unable
to bear the sight of the terrible farewell. He
is summoned by Oedipus to give his hand
in token of his promise to care for the help-
less girls. The children fall back, the blind
man waits with outstretched hand, and Creon
slowly and sadly walks across the stage and
gives the sign. Then Oedipus turns again to
his little ones. The painful scene, however,
has lasted long enough, and Creon orders

PLATE **XV.**

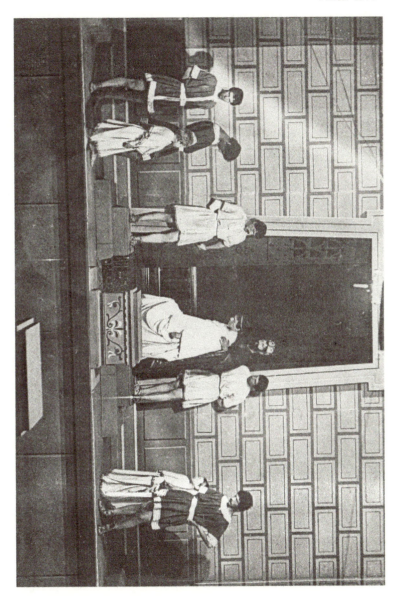

Oedipus to leave his children and withdraw.
It is a dreadful separation, but the king's
order is imperative. So Oedipus tears himself away, his attendants throw open the
doors, the attendants of Creon take the children by the hand, and Creon himself leads
Oedipus up the steps and into the palace.
(Plate XV.) The children and the second
messenger follow; the attendants of Oedipus
enter last and gently close the doors.

The music sounds again in pathetic tones,
and the Coryphaeus expresses for his fellows
the lesson of life.

> " Ye men of Thebes, behold this Oedipus,
>   Who knew the famous riddle and was noblest,
>   Whose fortune who saw not with envious glances ?
>   And, lo ! in what a sea of direst trouble
>   He now is plunged. From hence the lesson learn ye,
>   To reckon no man happy till ye witness
>   The closing day ; until he pass the border
>   Which severs life from death, unscathed by sorrow." *

With bowed heads the old men of Thebes
retire to the city, and the play is over. There

* Plumptre's translation.

is a moment's silence, and then the theatre rings with applause. It seems inappropriate, however, and ceases almost as suddenly as it began. The play has left such a solemn impression that the usual customs seem unfitting, and the audience disperses quietly.

A few minutes later the theatre is in darkness, and the actors go home not wholly certain of the result of their long task.

The newspapers of the following morning set all doubts at rest, and showed the fulfilment of all hopes.

———

From the " Boston Daily Advertiser."

In all simplicity and sincerity we say there can be no doubt that the performance was remarkably successful, and afforded great and peculiar pleasure to a critical audience. . . Here everything conspired in a wonderful way, the drama itself having such imaginative vividness, and every detail of representation being carried out with dignity, absolute precision and accuracy, and with a wonderful smoothness, resulting from most careful preparation under most competent and learned instructors. From the moment when, near the close of the instrumental introduction, the company of suppliants made their slow entrance from the right, and passing through the orchestra to the left, mounted the stage and laid their votive offerings on the altars before the palace, many a spectator must have forgotten his country and century, and have felt himself a Greek of the Greeks. Quite aside, also, from the acting and music, the great beauty of the correct costumes, and the fine *tableaux vivants* made by the groups of players was a feast to the eye and fancy throughout the evening. The acting as a whole was remarkably and surprisingly good. Most of the players were only amateurs, and of course showed their want of professional training; but there was extraordinarily little of immaturity in performance, both as to quality and as to quantity, considering the circumstances of the occasion."

From the Boston "Evening Transcript": —

"The production of the Oedipus Tyrannus of Sophocles at Cambridge, last night, was as brilliant a success in every way as could have been desired. Indeed, there was scarcely room for any miscarriage, so carefully and thoroughly had everything been prepared during the past six months. With a clear conception as to what was to be done, with practically unlimited means at command for its execution, and with the resources of the University in the way of young men of character and brain to draw on for talent and self-sacrificing labor, and learned scholars for counsel and training, this triumph was almost assured in advance. It is on all hands pronounced the most perfect and worthy reproduction of Greek drama in modern times. The *éclat* of the occasion, though not exceeding its merits, resounds throughout the country. The leading journals have been represented at the last rehearsal and first performance by special correspondents, and their elaborate accounts have been printed, accompanied by editorial comments, showing that the unique interest and importance of the event have been fully appreciated beyond the circle of the community of Boston and Cambridge."

From the "Boston Journal."

"The first public performance of the Oedipus Tyrannus of Sophocles, at Sanders Theatre, Cam-

bridge, last evening, was also the first performance of
this play in its original language in recent times, and
the first presentation of a Greek drama in this country. The event was therefore interesting for its
novelty, as well as for its dramatic and scholastic
importance. Its success was pronounced and instant ;
and indeed it may be doubted if a Greek play has
ever been so thoroughly well presented since the
times and audiences for which it was originally
written. . . . The production was a perfect one in
every detail, being throughout consistent, dignified,
strong, and fully accordant in earnest spirit with
all we have heretofore conceived of the realities
of the Greek stage. . . . It is an increasing matter of
marvel to all who will consider it, that this play has
ever been produced, even with the great resources at
the command of Harvard College."

From the Boston " Evening Traveller " : —

" The performance of the Oedipus, last night, at
Cambridge, brought delight to an immense and critical audience, and was a surprise, as we are disposed
to think, even to those who expected most. A distinguished scholar was heard to say to a friend, as

the great assembly broke up, — almost unwillingly,
— that it was itself an education to have witnessed
the spectacle. That was the feeling certainly among
the great body of the audience. They knew, for the
first time, what the classical tragedy is ; and entered,
for the first time, into the temper and the enthusiasm of the people who, in its day, applauded it so
eagerly."

From the special correspondent of the New
York " Nation " : —

" It was my good fortune last summer to witness
the performance of the Agamemnon of Aeschylus
in the hall of Balliol College, and it is natural that
on this occasion my thoughts should go back to that
scene, of which I endeavored at the time to give some
slight account to the readers of the ' Nation.' A comparison of the two performances is evidently unfair.
The Agamemnon and the Oedipus belong to different
stages of art. The articulation of the Oedipus is complete in itself. The Agamemnon is one of a trilogy,
and the choral masses demand a different disposition.
It would have been impossible to handle them as Mr.
Paine handles the choruses of the Oedipus, without

wearying the audience and dulling the edge of the
action.   Parts of them were sung, parts declaimed,
now in unison, now by single *choreutai*, and a certain
dramatic effect was thus attained, and a far closer
unity of actors and chorus than was possible in the
Harvard rendering of the Oedipus.   The antique
character was more seriously compromised, but the
vitality was more tense.   Nor would it be fair to
compare the external conditions.   The Oxford men
had made no long and elaborate preparation.   The
stage appliances were simple in the extreme.   Not
half as many shillings were spent at Oxford as dollars at Harvard.   A superb young undergraduate
was busy stencilling a part of the palace roof of the
Atreidae a couple of hours before the performance
began.   The costumes were not elaborate ; there
was no 'book of the opera,' no distinct effort to
be scholarly or archaeological ; and yet it was a
marked success, — a success that repeated itself at
Harrow, at Eton, in London.   It is a beautiful thing
to remember, with all its youthful dash and zest.
Carefully planned, thoroughly studied, wrought out
with minute attention to such details as fell within
the limits, our Harvard Oedipus was by far the more

finished piece of work, and the memory of it is a more brilliant picture."

From the " New York Times ": —

" The brilliant success of this attempt to put before an American audience a Greek tragedy in its original setting is a deserved reward for the unsparing labor and zeal of those who have taken part in the enterprise."

From the New York " Christian Union."

" The brilliant audiences, representative of the best American scholarship, which have gathered here, coming with mingled feelings of curiosity and scholarly interest to be amused and entertained by a representation of classic life, have been startled at first by the perfect and beautiful movement of the drama, and then irresistibly held in breathless attention upon the unfolding of a tragedy so full of human interest that, although spoken in a dead language, it is as contemporaneous as Hamlet or Faust."

From the " Springfield Republican " : —

" The Harvard students made of the Oedipus Tyrannus to-night something more than a play for the
closet and class-room. Their thoroughly dramatic
interpretation of the tragedy gave it a living and
human interest, and they had the sympathy and
fixed attention of every person from first to last.
The representation was a wonderfully accurate copy
of Attic models. In the pronunciation of the language, costumes, stage scenery, and choral effects,
it was doubtless the most faithful reproduction of a
play in the Dionysiac Theatre, at Athens, 2300 years
ago, that has ever been attempted in modern times."

From the Boston " Evening Transcript " of a later date : —

" The Greek play at Harvard is to be performed
for the last time this evening. The premium on the
price of the seats shows the eagerness to witness this
rare, noble, and beautiful effort in art. It seems a
pity that all is to be a memory only after this performance, and that so complete and worthy a presentation of the great Greek drama will never be seen
again, by this generation, at least. Yet the public of

Boston, whose fame as an art centre is still further magnified to the world by the triumph at the Harvard theatre, will not be unreasonable or ungrateful. It has only thanks and honor for the generous youths and the accomplished men who have given so much wearing labor to the production that there is no one of them but says that, if it were to be done over again, no possible rewards would tempt him to engage in it."

VI.

THE Harvard Greek play is over; the labors of many months have been brought to a conclusion more successful than any one had hoped; there is everything to remember with pride, and little or nothing to regret. In looking back one recalls with pleasure the devotion of those who took charge, the enthusiasm of the performers, and the quick response of the public. An impulse has been given to classical studies, and already two Greek plays are announced from other colleges. There is no ground for fear that the event will be forgotten. To those who witnessed the play, it will remain a memorable incident; to those who made the play, it will constitute one of the privileges of life.

There is, however, a feature of the play which is of more importance than all its pleasing memories. *Athenae omnium doctrinarum inventrices*, said the Roman orator; and among these the most prominent is a certain *doctrina vivendi*, which was the mother of all the excellences of that glorious age. In the play of Oedipus the King this doctrine is presented by a master's hand, and though the labor of production was so absorbing, and though the performance was so dazzling, yet the underlying moral significance did not go unheeded.

The Oedipus is a powerful exhibition of the fact that our lives " do ride upon a dial's point." Who could have foreseen the woes of Oedipus? As little can any man foresee his own. The sword is hanging, the shears of the weird sisters are moving across the web, the message is preparing, and no man knows when or how it shall be delivered. But there is a deeper moral in the play than this universal truth. Each man bears the responsibility not only of his own deeds, but also of the deeds of a long line of ancestors. "God does not pay at the end of every day, my Lord Cardinal," was said to Richelieu by one of his victims, " but at the end God pays." Every sin brings suffering, but not to the doer alone. This is the great moral basis of life, and it is a fact which will be enforced by the new ethics as it never was by the old. Some one has wittily said that we may be the sons of our grandfathers ; we certainly bear the consequences of their sins. Thebes weeps for the sins of her rulers. The suffering does not always fall upon the doer of the sin, but fall it does somewhere, and life would be a mockery if anything could be found to break the fall. There may be delay, there may be apparent miscarriage, but the sequence is inevitable.

"Sorrow tracketh wrong
As echo follows song,
On, on for ever."

To trace the working of the curse in the
family of Laius is enough to cause a shud-
der of apprehension, for the experience of
most men furnishes something similar at
least in kind.

It is obviously just to the fathers that their
sins should be visited upon their children, but
it is equally clear that it is hard upon the
children. The consequences of sin are as
careless of their object as is the rain. Oedipus was essentially an innocent man. To do
right is not sufficient to prevent suffering, if
some one before us has done wrong. This
is a fact painful to face, but out of the pain
grows the lesson. The laws which work for
the greatest happiness of the greatest number — if, indeed, there be such laws — are
not considerate of the happiness of any individual. This is the truth in the doctrine

of fate : every sin committed will be expi-
ated to the full by the innocent perhaps, by
the guilty assuredly. The Greek recognition
of this supreme fact is shown in the instant
acceptance·by Oedipus of the punishment of
sins in which he had no part. He is a man,
and he is willing to share the lot of human-
ity. It is this which redeems him from his
passion in the murder of Laius and the injustice toward Creon ; it is this which lifts him
to a truly tragic place, and entitles him to
the sympathies of mankind.

The performance of a Greek tragedy to-
day has two aspects, — the one, that of a
drama — δρᾶμα meaning a great action —
exhibiting in unmistakable outlines the in-
flexibility of the moral law ; the other, that
of an undertaking with no significance beyond
its interest. Since the circumstances of the
present day are such as are likely to render
the latter aspect the more common one, this

account of the Harvard Greek play may be
closed with an appeal.

> " Be otherwise instructed, you !
> And preferably ponder, ere ye pass,
> Each incident of this strange human play."

Appendix I.

—◆◆◆—

THE OEDIPUS TYRANNUS OF SOPHOCLES

will be performed in the original Greek at HARVARD UNIVERSITY, in the SANDERS THEATRE, on the evenings of May 17, 19, and 20. The part of Oedipus will be taken by MR. GEORGE RIDDLE, instructor in Elocution, and the other parts by students of the University. The music for the choruses has been composed for this performance by PROFESSOR J. K. PAINE; and the choral odes will be sung by a dramatic chorus of fifteen students, assisted by a supplementary chorus composed chiefly of graduates, with orchestral accompaniment.

Five hundred tickets for the first performance, at $3.00 each, and eight hundred for each of the other performances, at $2.00 each, will be offered to the public. Each ticket will entitle the holder to a reserved seat.

Of these tickets a number not exceeding 100 for the first evening and 200 for each of the succeeding evenings will be assigned by the committee to persons living in places distant from Cambridge. Applications for these may be made to MR. C. W. SEVER, University Bookstore, Cambridge, and must be received by him on or before March 25. These tickets will be assigned by lot, and adjacent seats (when desired) will be given to each applicant. If more tickets are asked for than can be assigned in this way, the committee will distribute those which are at their disposal to the applicants according to their judgment. All applicants will be informed immediately by mail of the number of tickets assigned them; and payment for the tickets will be deferred until such notice is received.

The regular sale of tickets will begin at the University Bookstore in Cambridge, and at 146 Tremont Street in Boston, on Monday, April 4, at 10 A.M.

The text of the Oedipus Tyrannus, in Greek and English, will be for sale at both places at which tickets are sold; and will be sent by mail to any address. Price, 50 cents; by mail, 60 cents.

The music of the choruses, composed by PROFESSOR

PAINE, with Greek and English words and piano accompaniment, will be published March 30 by MR. ARTHUR P. SCHMIDT, 146 Tremont Street, Boston, who will send it by mail on receipt of the price, $1.25.

W W GOODWIN, ⎫   *Committee*
J. W. WHITE,   ⎬   *of*
J. K. PAINE,   ⎭ *Arrangements.*

HARVARD UNIVERSITY,
    March 16, 1881.

Appendix 2.

ΠΑΣΙ ΤΟΙΣ ΘΕΩΜΕΝΟΙΣ ΧΑΙΡΕΙΝ

χαίρετ᾽ ἀστικὸς λεὼς,
ἴκταρ ἥμενοι Διὸς,
παρθένου φίλας φίλοι,
σωφρονοῦντες ἐν χρόνῳ.
Παλλάδος δ᾽ ὑπὸ πτεροῖς
ὄντας ἅζεται πατήρ.

ΣΟΦΟΚΛΕΟΥΣ

ΟΙΔΙΠΟΥΣ ΤΥΡΑΝΝΟΣ

ΔΙΔΑΧΘΗΣΕΤΑΙ ΕΝ ΘΕΑΤΡΩΙ ΤΩΙ ΤΟΥ ᾽ΑΡΒΑΡΔΙΟΥ ΔΙΔΑΣΚΑΛΕΙΟΥ

τῇ ἑβδόμῃ ἐπὶ δέκα τοῦ Θαργηλιῶνος μηνὸς, ἔτει /ΑΩΙΙΑ, καὶ αὖθις
τῇ ἐνάτῃ ἐπὶ δέκα καὶ τῇ εἰκάδι καὶ τῇ δεκάτῃ φθίνοντος,
καὶ τελευταῖον τῇ τετράδι φθίνοντος.

ΤΑ ΤΟΥ ΔΡΑΜΑΤΟΣ ΠΡΟΣΩΠΑ.

Οἰδίπους, Θηβαίων βασιλεύς	GEORGE RIDDLE.
᾽Ιερεὺς Διός	WILLIAM HOBBS MANNING.
Κρέων, ἀδελφὸς ᾽Ιοκάστης	HENRY NORMAN.
Τειρεσίας, μάντις τυφλός.	CURTIS GUILD.
᾽Ιοκάστη, Θηβαίων βασίλεια.	LEONARD ECKSTEIN OPDYCKE.
῎Αγγελος Κορίνθιος	ARTHUR WELLINGTON ROBERTS.
Θεράπων Λαΐου	GARDINER MARTIN LANE.
᾽Εξάγγελος	OWEN WISTER.

ΚΩΦΑ ΠΡΟΣΩΠΑ.

᾽Ακόλουθοι Οἰδίποδος	J. R. COOLIDGE, E. J. WENDELL.
᾽Ακόλουθοι ᾽Ιοκάστης	J. J. GREENOUGH, W. L. PUTNAM.
᾽Ακόλουθοι Κρέοντος	G. P. KEITH, J. LEE.
Παῖς Τειρεσίαν εἰσάγων	C. H. GOODWIN.
᾽Αντιγόνη	E. MANNING.
᾽Ισμήνη	J. K. WHITTEMORE.

᾽Ικέται. —G. P. KEITH, G. D. MARKHAM (ἱερῆς). W. H. HERRICK,
J. LEE, E. LOVERING, H. PUTNAM, L. A. SHAW, C. M.
WALSH (ἤθεοι λεκτοί). C. H. GOODWIN, E. MANNING,
R. MANNING, W. MERRILL, E. R. THAYER, J. K. WHIT-
TEMORE (παῖδες).

ΧΟΡΟΣ ΓΕΡΟΝΤΩΝ ΘΗΒΑΙΩΝ.

Κορυφαῖος. . . . . . Louis Butler McCagg.

Συγχορευτὴς ἐν τῷ τρίτῳ στασίμῳ μονῳδῶν . George Laurie Osgood.

Χορευταί —

N. M. Brigham,   Marshall H. Cushing,   Charles S. Hamlin,
Frederick R. Burton,   Wendell P. Davis,   Jared S. How,
Henry G. Chapin,   Morris Earle,   Howard Lilienthal,
Sumner Coolidge,   Percival J. Eaton,   Charles F. Mason,
    Edward P. Mason,   Gustavus Tuckerman.

Χοροδιδάσκαλος ὁ τὰς αὐλῳδίας ποιήσας . John Knowles Paine.

Ὑποβολεύς   George L. Kittredge.

Ἡ μὲν σκηνὴ τοῦ δράματος πρὸ τῶν βασιλείων ἐν Θήβαις ταῖς Βοιω-
τικαῖς ὑπόκειται. Ὁ δὲ χορὸς συνέστηκεν ἐκ Θηβαίων γερόντων. Προ-
λογίζει δ' Οἰδίπους.

Ἀξιοῦσιν οἱ ἐπιμεληταὶ πάντας τοὺς θεωροῦντας διαμένειν καθημένους
ἕως ἂν τελευτηθῶσιν οἱ ἐξόδιοι νόμοι. Εὐθὺς δ' ἀσθέντος τοῦ τετάρτου
στασίμου (ἰὼ γενεαὶ βροτῶν, κ. τ. ἑ.) ἀνάπαυσις γενήσεται τοῖς ἐξιέναι
βουλομένοις. Μετὰ δὲ ταῦτα αἱ θύραι κεκλείσονται.

Μετὰ τὴν θέαν ἅμαξαι ἱπποσιδηροδρομικαὶ ἕτοιμαι ἔσονται τοῖς ἐς
ἄστυ πορεύεσθαι μέλλουσιν.

Μετεφράσθη ἔνια χάριν τῶν μὴ ἑλληνιζόντων —

The spectators are urgently requested to remain seated until the end of the
orchestral postlude. A short pause will be made after the last choral song
(ἰὼ γενεαὶ βροτῶν, *O tribes of living men*, etc.) for the convenience of those who
wish to leave the theatre, and the doors will then remain closed until the end
of the performance.

Horse-cars will be ready after the performance for those who wish to go to
Boston.

Οὐιλσῶνες τύποις ἔγραψαν.

Appendix 3.

---·∞·---

A PARTIAL BIBLIOGRAPHY OF THE HARVARD GREEK PLAY.

[The names of the writers are given when known. An asterisk indicates that the date is given approximately.]

Accounts previous to the performances : —

Boston Sunday Herald. By H. Norman . .	Mar.	27
New York Herald. By H. Norman . .	Apr.	1
" " Evening Post . . . . "	16
Boston Daily Advertiser	May	2
Boston Daily Advertiser. An account of the music by G. A. Burdett . . . . "	5
Boston Daily Advertiser · . . . "	11
Chicago Tribune* . . . . . "	14
The Harvard Register. By Prof. J. W. White	May	
Boston Journal	May	17
" Post . . . . . . "	
" Traveller · . . . . . "	
Philadelphia Telegraph . . . "	
Brooklyn Times . . "	
The Nation. By Prof. B. L. Gildersleeve of Johns Hopkins University "	

Reports of the Rehearsal : —

 New York Sun .   .   .   . May 15
 Boston Daily Advertiser   .   .   .   . May 16
  " Transcript   .   .   .   .   . "
  " Herald   .   .   .   .   .   . "
  " Globe   .   .   .   .   .   . "
 New York Tribune   .   .   .   .   . "
  " " Evening Post   .   .   .   . "

Reports of the Performance : —   .

 Boston Daily Advertiser   .   .   .   . May 18
  " " Herald .   .   .   .   . "
  " " Journal   .   .   .   . "
  " " Post   .   .   .   .   . "
  " " Globe   .   .   .   . "
  " " Transcript   .   .   . "
  " " Traveller .   .   .   . "
 New York Sun .   .   .   .   . "
  " " Times   .   .   .   . "
  " " World. By F. Marion Crawford   . "
  " " Herald .   .   .   .   . "
  " " Courier (criticism of the music) ·   . "
 Chicago Tribune   .   .   .   .   . "
 Baltimore Sun   .   .   .   .   .   . "
 Harvard Lampoon†   .   .   .   . "
 New Haven Union   .   .   .   ·   . "
 Philadelphia Bulletin   .   .   .   . "
 Pittsburg Dispatch   .   .   .   . . May 19
 Springfield Republican* .   .   .   . "

† With this exception the Harvard papers are not mentioned, as references to the play were contained in almost every issue during April and May. See the Echo, Crimson, Advocate, and Lampoon.

Worcester Spy .   .   .   . May 19
New York Star .   .   .   .   .   .   "
Philadelphia News* .   .   .   .   .   "
New Haven Palladium* .   .   .   .   .   "
Providence Journal* .   .   .   .   .   "
Wilmington (Del.) Every Evening*   .   May 21
Literary World .   .   .   .   .   .   "
The New York Critic. By Mrs. Julia Ward
    Howe   .   .   .   .   "
New York Independent. By Rev. Kinsley
    Twining .   .   .   . May 22
Providence Press* .   .   .   .   .   .   "
Hartford Courant   .   .   .   .   .   . May 23
Brooklyn Eagle.* By Rev. J. W. Chadwick .   "   24
New York Christian Union. By H. W. Mabie . May 25
Boston Congregationalist   .   .   .   .   "
The Nation. By Prof. B. L. Gildersleeve of
    Johns Hopkins University   .   .   . May 26
Harper's Weekly, with six illustrations. By Prof.
    Louis Dyer   .   .   .   . May 28

Incidental discussions of the play : —
    Boston Advertiser   .   .   .   .   May 18 and 19
        "   Transcript .   .   .   .   .   May 20
        "   "   .   .   .   .   .   "   21
    Literary World   .   .   .   .   .   June 4

The Atlantic Monthly. By Prof. C. E. Norton . July, 1881
The Century Magazine. An account of the costumes,
    by F. D. Millet   .   .   .   .   November, 1881

For EU product safety concerns, contact us at Calle de José Abascal, 56–1°,
28003 Madrid, Spain or eugpsr@cambridge.org.